Tip the Hen

By Debbie Croft

I can see Tip.

Tip is a hen.

Tip is my pet hen.

Tip has a pen.

I can pat Tip in the pen.

Pat, pat, pat!

Tip has a pan in her pen.

Tip can sip at the pan.

Sip, Tip, sip!

Tip can sit in her pen.

Tip sits, sits, sits!

CHECKING FOR MEANING

1. Who is the main character in the story? *(Literal)*

2. Where does Tip live? *(Literal)*

3. Do you think Tip likes sitting in her pen? Why? *(Inferential)*

EXTENDING VOCABULARY

can	Look at the word *can.* Can you think of other words that rhyme with *can*?
hen	Look at the word *hen.* Look back at the story. Can you find any other words that rhyme with *hen*?
pen	Look at the word *pen.* What is the first sound in this word? What other words can you think of that begin with this sound?

MOVING BEYOND THE TEXT

1. What might happen to Tip if she didn't have a pen?

2. How do you think Tip feels when her owner pats her in the pen? Why?

3. How can we take care of our pets and make sure they feel safe and happy?

SPEED SOUNDS

| Cc | Bb | Rr | Ee | Ff | Hh | Nn |

| Mm | Ss | Aa | Pp | Ii | Tt |

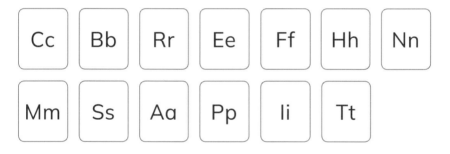

PRACTICE WORDS

can

hen

pet

in

pen

pan